Somewhere Down the Road

By Debbie Kitchings

PublishAmerica
Baltimore

Aug '08

© 2008 by Debbie Kitchings.
All rights reserved. No part of this book may be reproduced, stored in a retrieval system or transmitted in any form or by any means without the prior written permission of the publishers, except by a reviewer who may quote brief passages in a review to be printed in a newspaper, magazine or journal.

First printing

To Ethel
May all your dreams come true Somewhere Down the Road
Debbie Kitchings

PublishAmerica has allowed this work to remain exactly as the author intended, verbatim, without editorial input.

ISBN: 1-60563-655-X
PUBLISHED BY PUBLISHAMERICA, LLLP
www.publishamerica.com
Baltimore

Printed in the United States of America

I dedicate this book to my mother and sister for their support that made this book a reality and my dear friends who have encouraged me throughout this project.

I also dedicate this book to the memory of my daddy, Grover Kitchings.

Acknowledgments

The successful completion of this book belongs to my family and friends. Without their support, encouragement, and enthusiasm, this book would have remained just a dream.

I would like to thank my mother, Eva Kitchings, and my sister, Linda Whilden for their support and patience throughout this process. I have had to work many long hours to complete this book of poems and they never complained about the time I had to spend working. In fact, they helped however they could. You will never know how much I love and appreciate you.

I would also like to thank my friends who encouraged me to get my work published. I never would have sent my work in for publication without your encouragement. You have also encouraged me to write and always provided me positive feedback about my poems.

I thank God for letting this dream become a reality. I know that without Him I am nothing, but with God all things are possible. I thank God for this blessing he has given me.

Lastly, I would like to thank PublishAmerica for giving me this chance. I could not have found a nicer group of people to work with. Thank you so much for your help and support.

Spirits on the Beach

On the beach by the sea,
I saw a little girl that looked just like me.
Gathering seashells out of the sand,
Holding them gently in her little hand.

Suddenly she stood up and turned around,
And without making a sound,
She waved at me, then with a smile,
She disappeared for a little while.

I sat on the beach wondering what she wanted,
Why am I suddenly being haunted?
And why do my eyes fill with tears,
When she suddenly disappears?

I sat in the sand pondering this,
When she appeared and gave me a kiss.
And whispered, "Come play with me,
In the sand by the sea."

We built a castle in the sand,
And pretended we were kings of the land.
We laughed and played all through the day,
I never thought it would be this way.

When the sun was setting low,
The little girl said she must go.
I begged her not to leave me there,
To be alone again I could not bear.

I had not laughed since that dreadful day,
When my husband and child went away.
On that cold, dreary, rainy night,
The plane did not complete its flight.

The sunshine left my life that year,
And only today did it reappear.
The little girl said she understood,
She would help me if she could.

She took my hand as we walked along,
And she sang me a little song.
A song of life that is full and complete,
A life full of happiness and love so sweet.

Then she disappeared from my sight,
And I walked alone into the night.
Thinking about what she had said,
I walked home and went to bed.

I dreamed of the night I was wed,
And of the wonderful life I had led.
With my baby so soft and sweet,
Its curly hair and tiny feet.

Then I saw my husband and child up above,
Sending me all of their love,
From the heavens in the sky,
I'll be with them by and by.

When I woke up the sun was shining bright,
And with the dawn I saw the light.
I must learn to live again,
Sharing as much love as I possibly can.

Castles in the Sky

I see a castle in the sky,
Floating in the air so high.
Above the white and fluffy cloud,
Standing so tall and proud.

I see a bird flying through the air,
And into the castle window to share.
The news of the land down below,
And of all the earth has to show.

The prince of dreams jumped on his white horse,
He rode his stallion with such force.
To reach the earth at that special spot,
Where a cry for help had him brought.

Under the willow tree down by the lake,
A young girl's heart was about to break.
She was lost and all alone,
And didn't even notice that the bright sun shone.

The prince of dreams looked at her there,
Her blond curls fell over her skin so fair.
Her big blue eyes were full of tears,
And her heart full of fears.

The prince's heart melted at the sight,
Of the lovely girl in such a plight.
He waved his hand across the lake,
And a beautiful rainbow he did make.

Beautiful colors spread through the sky,
To the castle way up high.
Past the clouds in the sky so blue,
In a land where dreams do come true.

They rode off to that magical land,
And walked through the palace hand in hand.
Where the birds always sang and the sun always shined,
And everyone is always true and kind.

A Child's Smile

Have you ever had a day,
When all your skies were gray?
A day when nothing goes right,
And happiness seems out of sight.

And then you look at a child,
And see a smile so sweet and mild.
As if an angel from above,
Touched that child with His love.

The gray clouds seem to part,
And the day has a new start.
With sunshine and rainbows and colorful flowers,
And only an occasional summer shower.

Seasons

The autumn leaves of red and gold,
Are turning brown with the cold.
The cold north wind blows them to the ground,
Where they fall without a sound.

The snow begins to softly fall,
Upon the trees standing tall.
The ground is covered with a sheet of white,
Which sparkles even during the night.

The snow melts into spring,
The sound of birds begins to ring.
Baby animals suddenly appear,
Under a sky that is blue and clear.

Summer is hot and dry,
Very few clouds are in the sky.
The days are long, the sun is bright,
The lakes are warm even at night.

I Believe

I believe in unicorns and castles in the sky,
And I believe that fairies sprinkle moonbeams as they fly.
I believe in elves that dance sprightly through the night,
And I believe fireflies are lanterns to give them light.

I believe in love that is always pure and good,
A love where people really care and always understood.
I believe in a love that last through the age of time,
Even when the road is rough and often an uphill climb.

I believe in the magic of a little child,
We could learn a lot from someone so meek and mild.
They know how to give their heart with a hug and a smile,
A very special kind of love that knows how to last a while.

Morning Happiness

The morning dawns bright and clear,
The birds are singing of the day that is here.
The sun's warmth kisses my face,
And bathes the world in style and grace.

Dewdrops sparkle on the rose,
And a beautiful fragrance drifts up to my nose.
The gentle breeze blows through my hair,
To wash away all my cares.

Happiness is here and now,
I just wish that I knew how,
To make it last through the day,
And push all my troubles away.

The Old Violin

The old violin hung on the wall,
Secured by a nail so it wouldn't fall.
It was covered in dust so it had lost its shine,
No one remembered its music so fine.

The old violin remembered a time long ago,
When it was new and still had its bow.
A little boy was full of delight,
The first time the violin came into his sight.

The violin barely fit under his little chin,
The bow was too long and the boy's fingers too thin.
The little boy played the violin with delight,
Even though the sound was not quite right.

The little boy played his violin every day,
And the squeaks and squawks went away.
In its place came a beautiful sound,
That touched every heart that it found.

Time went by and the boy fell in love,
His music drifted to her on the wings of a dove.
He won her heart with his violin,
A violin that had won his heart when he was only ten.

They married and had such a wonderful life,
Violin music lessened their stress and their strife.
Their family grew when they had two little girls,
They had big blue eyes and dark brown curls.

The violin was still a big part of the boy,
It played lively music while the girls danced with joy.
And when it was time for the girls to go to bed,
The soft music it played made sweet dreams in their head.

The violin played when his daughters wed,
The violin kept him company after his wife was dead.
The violin's music grew sweeter through the years,
It could bring you laughter or it could bring you tears.

Years went by, and he joined his dear wife,
The violin was left behind to lead a lonely life.
No beautiful music comes from the violin,
It is old and scratched and covered in rosin.

One of the daughters hung it on the wall,
To remember her dad when he was young and tall.
She loved to listen when he played,
She loved the beautiful music he made.

One day his great grandson saw the violin,
The young lad was only ten.
The little boy was full of delight,
The first time the violin came into sight.

His grandmother told her of another boy,
That played the violin and brought everyone joy
She told him of the music he would play,
How he cherished that violin each and every day.

She got the violin down and found the old bow,
Dusted it off to make the finish glow.
She handed the violin to her grandson that day,
Knowing her dad would want it that way.

The old violin makes music once more,
It no longer considers life a bore.
It is bringing people laughter and tears,
With the music it has played throughout the years.

The Snow

The snow silently falls through the cold winter night,
It glistens brightly in the morning light.
A soft white blanket covers the ground,
As the snow falls without making a sound.

The soft white snow looks like the gown of a bride,
So soft and pure and worn with pride.
The snowflakes are like the delicate lace,
That covers a blushing bride's beautiful face.

There is not a sound to be heard,
No cars passing by or the song of a bird.
The icicles glisten brightly in the sun,
The trees droop from the ice as if it weighed a ton.

The earth is quiet and very still,
Except for the children's squeal.
When they wake to see the beautiful snow,
They can't wait to get dressed and go.

Mom makes sure they wear plenty of clothes,
To keep them warm when the north wind blows.
They roll the snow to make a large snowman,
And dress him in the clothes of a man.

Then the children start throwing snowballs,
They are pretty cold and wet by the time their mother calls.
She has hot chocolate waiting to warm them up,
It has many marshmallows in the top of the cup.

The ice has broken the electric lines,
The limb broke off one of the big pines.
Mom gets out one of the old oil lamps,
That they used when they build a camp.

The telephone is out and the water pipes have froze,
There is nothing to do but sit in front of the fire and doze.
Wrapped in blankets in front of the fireplace,
The family sings songs, play games, and talk face to face.

The next day is warm and the snow will melt,
But the fun shared by the family will still be felt.
Memories of this day will hold a special place in their heart,
A day spent having fun with family even when they have grown apart.

First Love

I saw her under an old oak tree,
She suddenly looked up and smiled at me.
With a smile that lit up her face,
I felt my heart start to race.

I looked into her gentle warm eyes,
That sparkled like the stars in the sky.
She was a lady of elegance and grace,
A beautiful creature dressed in white lace.

Her honey gold hair looked like silk,
Her complexion was of peaches and milk.
I never believed in love at first sight,
But I felt in my heart that this love was right.

Your Gift of Music

Your music brings me beauty, your music brings me song,
Your music brings me warmth when the nights are cold and long.
Your music fills my heart and soul until it overflows,
Your music fills me with happiness and makes me forget my woes.

Your music fills my empty life with love and faith and hope,
And when troubles fill my life, your music helps me cope.
Your music is so beautiful that tears come to my eyes,
As you sing of lost loves and broken hearts and I hear your sighs.

Your music is a gift from God that you share with me,
A precious gift to a stranger that you will never see.
How do I thank you for a gift so precious and so rare,
A special gift given with love and tender care.

The Pup

The family dog disappeared and can't be found,
She's hidden under the porch not making a sound.
Five little pups with their eyes closed tight,
They are such an adorable sight.

Time goes by and the pups come toddling out,
The children see them and give a shout.
They play and they scamper throughout the day,
"What will we do with them?" the parents say.

Four of the puppies are finally given away,
One little pup seems bound to stay.
No more friends need another pet,
The needs of this pup just can't be met.

The family decides they don't need another pet,
So on a day when it is so cold and wet,
They take the dog down a country road,
A long lonely road where no house abode.

The poor little pup was dumped out right there,
The family did it without a thought or a care.
The little pup did not know what to do,
As the car drove off without further ado.

The pup was hungry, cold, and scared,
The pup just sat in the road and stared,
At where the car and his family had disappeared,
And that it wasn't coming back was what he feared.

He looked for a warm place to sleep under a tree,
The scary sounds around him made him want to flee.
His hunger got worse, but no food was in sight,
He looked hard for food, but couldn't find a bite.

Day after day and the pup grew thin,
Until one day he saw some men.
They picked him up and took him to a warm place,
To a nice lady named Lori with a very sweet face.

She gave the puppy some water and some food,
The little puppy had a full tummy and felt very good.
She gave the pup a nice soft warm bed,
And the pup laid down his tired little head.

The nice lady found the pup a new place to live,
With a little girl who had a lot of love to give.
Desert Paws give these animals a second chance to belong,
To a family that will spay and neuter and not do animals wrong.

The Manilow Fund for Health and Hope

A little boy comes home from school,
His report card this time was cool.
His mom is at the sink washing a dish,
On the stove she is cooking fish.

She just tells her son that he did fine,
And to go wash his hands and get ready to dine.
And as the dejected little boy walks past,
He sees a new black eye that's worse than the last.

His mom turns quietly around,
And the little boy leaves without making a sound.
He knows that the evening will be bad,
And the night will be long with his drunken dad.

And then across the busy street,
A little boy we will meet.
He was in a car wreak last year,
Losing him was the parents' greatest fear.

It took a blood transfusion to save the little boy,
But the tainted blood used took out all the joy.
The child now has to live with having AIDS,
The parents watch now as their child's life fades.

Down the street live little twin girls,
With beautiful blue eyes and golden curls.
One of the girls got very sick,
A lump on her side got very thick.

The doctor came out and shook his head,
The parents cried at what the doctor said.
The child has cancer and it looks very bad,
Everyone who knows her is very sad.

In a class sat a little boy,
His eyes glistened with joy.
As he listened about a chance to play,
A musical instrument in the band each day.

Then the teacher said each would have to pay,
To buy an instrument to get to play.
The little boy looked sadly down at his feet,
He knew this need he could not meet.

His worn shoes were already too tight,
And his single mom worked with all her might.
To keep food on the table and clothes on his back,
Extra money for an instrument they just couldn't hack.

One day there was a very talented man,
Who believed in doing all that he can.
To share his blessing with others around,
There are so many needs he has found.

He started a fund for the abused, sick, and poor,
For all of those people who wish for more.
He gives them hope for a better life,
He take away some of their stress and strife.

He gives these people a reason to live,
By being willing of himself to give.
He gives these people a reason to hope,
He gives these people a way to cope.

Spring

The sun comes out to warm the day,
The flowers are about in a pretty bouquet.
The sweet smell of roses drifts through the air,
With a fragrance so delicate and so rare.

Butterflies flit from flower to flower,
Flaunting their colors like a rainbow after a shower.
Baby bunnies play chase close to their nest,
Stopping only when they need to rest.

Baby birds are learning to fly,
You can hear their fear as they cry.
A mother bird gives the last baby a shove,
It falls from the nest then soars above.

After a long winter spring has finally come,
The bees are busy making honey as they hum.
The birds are singing songs of love,
For all these things thank God above.

Old Friends

Little girls not yet two,
All alone and feeling blue.
Until one day by fate they meet,
On a country road with little bare feet.

With just one look they suddenly knew,
This friendship was special even though it was new.
They played through the day with laughter and fun,
Until the sun set and the day was done.

The girls got older and started school,
They were shy and quiet and followed every rule.
The playground was their place to play,
They met there every single day.

One of the girls moved away for a while,
They were separated by many a mile.
But the friendship stayed just as strong,
A friendship like theirs always last long.

Then the girl moved back home one day,
It was as if they had never gone a separate way.
Older now they talked of clothes and boys,
They were now too old to play with toys.

They could spend hours talking about their dreams,
Anything was possible for them or so it seems.
They talked of the past and the future too,
They laughed and giggled all the day through.

As they grew up life took them separate ways,
Jobs in different places filled their days.
They still kept in touch through mutual friends,
This happens so often when school life ends.

New jobs took them both to a brand new place,
And to their delight they saw a familiar face.
The dear friends worked together next door,
They were so happy it made their hearts soar.

Now they work together each day,
They support each other in every way.
Joys and sorrows they always share,
And they always know they have a friend to care.

Their plans for the future as they grow old,
Include their friendship that has never grown cold.
Up until the life they know ends,
They will be the very best of friends.

Church on the Hill

The church on the hill is quite new,
The fresh white paint sparkles like the dew.
The stained glass windows are shiny and clean,
Casting the most beautiful colors ever seen.

The little church is filled with young and old,
This warm little church is never cold.
It is always filled with love for others,
The people consider each other sisters and brothers.

The people raise their voices in praise,
As they sing songs of God's loving ways.
The preacher is a pastor and also a friend,
They are his flock of sheep that he will always tend.

Children run and play at a church picnic,
Women take care of the elderly and sick.
Men move tables and cook on the grill,
Until everyone has eaten their fill.

Girls in white dresses walk down the aisle,
New babies are born after awhile.
Couples are married fifty years to the same mate,
These are reason for the church to celebrate.

When troubled times begin to fall,
There is always someone to call.
A church full of people who really care,
And willing to help with troubles friends bear.

A place to share good times and bad,
To laugh and cry or even feel sad.
A place to share God's precious love,
So one day we can meet in Heaven above.

A Teacher's Challenge

There was a young woman who worked at a school,
When she saw her thirty children she fell off her stool.
Their desks were lined up from wall to wall,
If any more children come, they will have to sit out in the hall.

Thirty hugs at the end of the day,
Thirty smiles all bright and gay.
Tears of pain from a skinned knee,
That feels all better with a kiss from me.

That many children keep me very busy,
I have so much to do that I feel dizzy,
But when they all have learned to read,
I feel like I have planted a little seed.

Daddy's Little Girl

Daddy's little girl is sitting in his lap,
While he sings lullabies to make her take a nap.
He rocks and sings quietly until she falls asleep,
And he is amazed the love he feels goes so deep.

She doesn't have to be talented or even very pretty,
She doesn't have to be smart or particularly witty.
Just being his little girl is more than enough,
His precious little girl doesn't need all that stuff.

Her daddy can do anything in her little eyes,
And he tries his best because he hates when she cries.
He builds dollhouses and fixes broken toys,
And dreads the day when she discovers boys.

She follows her daddy everywhere he goes,
And he tries his best to teach her all he knows.
They work on cars and plumbing and gardens in the yard,
She usually just hands him tools because the work is just too hard.

The girl grows up through the years,
Her daddy is there through her happy times and tears.
The love they share is very strong,
It is a love that will last a lifetime long.

When her daddy became sick and old,
Her love for him never grew cold.
Even though he lives in heaven the rest of his days,
She is still Daddy's little girl now and always.

West Rusk Elementary

West Rusk Elementary is a wonderful place,
The children are sweet and full of grace.
They always greet me with a smile and a wave,
And they at least try to behave.

The teachers are friendly and very kind,
A group like this is hard to find.
They are truly special in every way,
I know I will love them more each day.

Our principal is a wonderful leader,
She always supports us when we need her.
She lifts our spirits and fills us with pride,
We are happy to have her by our side.

I am glad to be a part of this,
The people here fill my life with bliss.
To the students, teachers, and principal too,
I'm so lucky to be a part of you.

A Woman's Dreams

In every woman is a beautiful princess,
She may be a mother, executive, or waitress.
Her life is usually busy and full of stress,
Taking care of everything and everyone else.

But when things slow down she stares into space,
And pictures herself beautiful and dressed in delicate white lace.
She sees a man brave, handsome, and strong,
Just looking at him fills her heart with a song.

He takes her burdens and problems she bears,
And all of her worries he is willing to share.
On his shoulder she rests her tired head,
And her problems just seem to have fled.

She feels so special encircled in his arms,
And she is not immune to all of his charms.
He looks at her with love and devotion,
She feels like she just drank a love potion.

Then the telephone rings loud and clear,
And the dreams are gone that she held so dear.
Back to the life she has always known,
Her troubles are hers to bear alone.

A Special Child

A special child enters a brand new place,
And looks up into a stranger's face.
Her little body tenses with fear,
And she tries real hard not to shed a tear.

This is her new class and teacher her parents say,
She wonders what happened to the one she had yesterday.
Nothing is familiar, nothing the same,
She no longer knows the rules of the game.

Everyone makes a fuss when she eats the glue,
And they take her crayons when she eats them too.
She drops her box and makes a mess,
How much trouble she's in now is only a guess.

To her surprise the teacher kneels down,
On her face is a smile instead of a frown.
She helps her clean up the mess that she made,
And the little girl's fears start to fade.

The teacher helps her learn right from wrong,
The little girl even learns to sing a new song.
She can't do the work that the others can do,
But she feels proud of what she is accomplishing too.

Each child is special in its own way,
Our job is to guide them each and every day.
God put his precious children in our care.
They are meant to be a blessing, not a burden to bear.

Lasting Love

They danced together in the bright moonlight,
Under the stars that twinkled in the night.
Crickets chirping were the only sound,
As he sang softly in her ear and twirled her around.

The love they share is so very real,
There are no words to describe how they feel.
They make the most of each moment together,
Whether life brings them sunshine or stormy weather.

When hard times and troubles do arise,
They try their best always to be wise.
Together they decide what they need to do,
Decisions are always best made by two.

They fill their lives with laughter, love, and fun.
Spending nights in each other's arms when the day is done.
They know that their love is here to stay,
Their love will last forever and a day.

A Mother's Love

There is no love more special than that of a mother,
It is a love that is more special than any other.
A mother's love is always there,
No matter what, she will always care.

She patches skinned knees with a bandage and a hug,
And doesn't fuss when something is spilled on the rug.
She is always there at recitals and school plays,
Even when she had other things to do on those days.

When the child's heart is broken and she is in tears,
Her mother is there to share the wisdom of her years.
As the daughter grows up and big decisions arise,
Her mother is there to give guidance and to advise.

A girl still needs her mother no matter how old she gets,
With her mother as her best friend she will have no regrets.
Through life they share laughter, joy, and tears,
But with her mother by her side she will have no fears.

Sisters

At times big sisters are quite bossy it seems,
But they also share your problems and dreams.
You can tell them a secret you would tell no other,
And know that the secret will go no further.

They help pass the time on long summer days,
Making life interesting in different ways.
Looking at the clouds to see what pictures we can find,
Taking walks in the woods with our dogs following behind.

My sister plays the piano while I sing along,
She has taught me almost every single song.
We catch fireflies in the middle of the night,
And we put them in a jar to look at their light.

We have tea parties with real cookies and tea,
There is always an extra cookie just for me.
We look in the road to collect pretty rocks,
We make funny puppets out of old socks.

We passed though our childhood with laughter and fun,
We have played in the rain and we have played in the sun.
Now we are grown and we no longer play,
But we are still close and that is how we will stay.

Sweethearts Forever

The woman sat in the old porch swing,
And looked at the plain gold band ring.
She remembered back through the years,
Of memories she holds so tender and dear.

She remembered when she was a young girl,
With dark brown hair that had a curl.
She remembered wearing pink ribbons and lace,
She was told she had pretty eyes and face.

She remembers when she met a young man one day,
He was so handsome that he took her breath away.
He looked at her and gave her a smile so sweet.
She was sure he would be able to hear her heart beat.

They took a long walk and talked for hours,
He stopped to pick her a bouquet of wildflowers.
After that they were seldom apart,
The young man had won her heart.

They were wed on the first day of June,
They danced together in the light of the moon.
When the groom gave his new bride a kiss,
They both knew they would always live in bliss.

A few years later their life would fill,
With beautiful children in the house on the hill.
Their life was filled with laughter and joy,
With one little girl and one little boy.

More years passed by and the children grew up,
The house felt empty so the couple got a pup.
He puttered in the garden and she learned to knit,
In the afternoons they went to the porch to sit.

They were still sweethearts even though they were old,
Their love for each other has never grown cold.
They still held hands and would steal a kiss,
And they still live their lives in marital bliss.

They never get tired of being together,
Holding hands and gazing at one another.
They still enjoyed when they went walking,
They were comfortable in silence or in talking.

Now the woman sits in the swing all alone,
With only her memories to carry her on.
Even though at times she will cry,
The love they shared will never die.

Little Things

What does my sweetheart love about me?
He loves the way I sing off key.
He loves when I dance around the room,
Sweeping and dancing with the broom.

He loves me when I'm in a pretty dress,
And he loves me when I look a mess.
He loves me in high heels and hose,
And he loves me in bare feet and toes.

When the warm sunshine makes me smile,
He takes time to walk with me for a while.
He says he loves the sun glistening in my hair,
As he touches it with such gentleness and care.

He loves the way I bring home a stray pet,
Although he always pretends to fret.
When he thinks I'm not looking I will see,
That he is petting and feeding the pet for me.

My sweetheart tells me what a lucky man he is,
To have a special woman like me that is all his.
My sweetheart doesn't know I'm the lucky one here,
He is really the special one and he is such a dear.

London School Explosion

It was in a small town in Texas in March 1937,
When a school full of children went to Heaven.
It was almost time for the school day to end,
The children were making plans with a friend.

They never knew the bell wouldn't ring that day,
The buses wouldn't run and they would never play.
That afternoon the children would have no fun,
The children's homework would never be done.

There was a gas leak but no one could tell,
No one had thought about making gas smell.
A flick of a simple light switch was all it took,
And the whole school building crumbled and shook.

The building came down upon them all,
On teachers and children it did fall.
Our dear children were crushed by debris,
Everyone offered their services free.

Men brought trucks to take those they had found,
To all of the hospitals in towns all around.
They dug and they worked and they cried at the scene,
For a generation of children that would never bee seen.

A whole generation lost to the small town,
Lives lost forever because a school fell down.
The people gathered together to mourn and to weep,
To find memories in the rubble that they could keep.

A memorial was set up in the middle of the street,
Dedicated to the lost lives and the children so sweet.
Once again the school is filled with children and laughter,
But those dear children will live in our hearts forever after.

Somewhere Down the Road

Somewhere down the road my dreams are alive,
My dreams are just waiting for me to arrive.
I will walk along a road that is unknown,
Sometimes with a friend and sometimes alone.

Parts of the road are filled with beauty and peace,
And will make me wish the road would never cease.
I will be happy and life will be good,
Everything in life will be as it should.

Other parts of the road will be rocky and an uphill climb,
It will seem I have sorrow instead of joy most of the time.
These hard times in life seem to make me strong,
Although I hope not to endure them for very long.

I will be a better person for the good times and the bad,
By being more compassionate when my friends are sad.
I will be truly happy when my friends succeed,
And they can count on me when they are in need.

I know this is a journey that I have to make,
A time when I must learn to give and learn to take.
When I reach the end of that long and winding road,
I will find my rainbow and where my dreams abode.

Birds of a Feather

A little yellow parrot lived in a pet store,
Sitting on a perch all day was quite a bore.
One day a woman came to look all around,
The little bird whistled making a pretty sound.

She stopped for a moment to talk to the bird,
Then she turned and left without another word.
The bird was not very happy at being ignored,
So with a flap of her wings through the air she soared.

She landed on her shoulder to continue her song,
With this woman is where she wanted to belong.
Before the woman left she was put back on her cage,
The little bird was unhappy and screamed with rage.

The woman came back quite often to buy fish for her tank,
And every time she left without her the little bird's heart sank.
When the woman walked in the store, the bird would call out,
Then she would jump on the woman's shoulder and ride about.

One day the woman came and talked to the clerk at the store,
The poor bird expected to be left there as had happened before.
The woman said the bird loved her and she loved the bird too,
And to live their lives together is what they should do.

She picked the bird up and cuddled it with care,
The bird chirped and preened the woman's long hair.
They bought a cage, bird toys and some food,
Life for the little bird was looking pretty good.

Now the bird is happy all through the day,
She eats at the table and usually gets her way.
The woman plays the violin and the bird sings,
While the bird rides the bow and flaps her wings.

The bird helps the woman when she cleans the house,
She helps to take unnecessary buttons off her blouse.
The little bird helps the woman oil paint and knit,
Then it is time for the bird to nap for a little bit.

The little bird has a home and no longer feels bored,
Now the bird has the woman that she has always adored.
The friendship between the two through the years has grown,
A friendship that was special and the bird had always known.

Autumn Fairies

The little fairies came out one crisp cool day,
After the summer's heat they were ready to play,
They found some paint of red, yellow, and gold,
And painted all the leaves colors bright and bold.

They shook the branches of the trees,
To make some leaves blow in the breeze.
That way the leaves would cover the ground,
With all of the colors that the fairies had found.

The fairies hid when people came by,
The people just stopped and gave a sigh.
The beauty was just breathtaking to see,
It lifted their spirits and made them feel free.

The fairies giggled when the children would rake,
And a huge stack of colorful leaves they would make.
Just so they could run and jump in the pile,
With plenty of giggles and grace and style.

The fairies saw these bright colored leaves,
That decorated the ground and all of the trees.
For one season this is what the people need,
To brighten their world all the fairies agreed.

So now every fall the fairies paint the world bright,
They gather their brushes and paint in the moonlight.
So the people will wake to a world of beauty and fun,
And enjoy all the hard work the fairies have done.

A Love Gone Wrong

A little girl plays with her dolls and dreams of her wedding day,
She dresses in her mother's clothes and the high heels make her sway.
She imagines walking down the aisle to meet her handsome groom,
In the early summer when the roses are in bloom.

The girl blossoms like a flower as she reaches her teen years,
She is not only beautiful but she is loved by all her peers.
One day she meets a boy who thinks she is so fine,
He loves the way her smile makes her eyes shine.

They went to the movies on Saturday night,
And he stole a kiss at every red light.
They fell in love and in the spring,
He surprised her with a diamond ring.

She had the wedding she had always dreamed of,
As they exchanged vows of their undying love.
The blushing bride was dressed in white lace,
The love they shared showed in her face.

Their house was small but full of laughter,
They knew they would live happily ever after.
Through their love several babies were born,
The last one died and together they did mourn.

After the death of a child no one is the same,
Even though no one is really to blame.
Laughter and fun is harder to come by,
And it is much easier for them to cry.

Instead of lovers they become father and mother,
They spent time with children instead of each other.
He works long hours so they can pay the bills,
She takes care of children and cleans up spills.

She no longer worries with her nails or hair,
Or takes the time to dress with the usual care.
He comes in late from work and is hungry and tired,
No longer paying attention to the wife he had admired.

Through the years they have grown apart,
They no longer talk about what's in their heart.
They talk about their problems that are very real,
But they never talk of romance or how they feel.

They find they fight more often than they did before,
They used to talk together and accomplished much more.
Little things that never seemed to matter all that much,
Now start a fight instead of love and a gentle touch.

They decide that maybe they should part,
Although it causes great pain in their heart.
Where is the love that they vowed in the past,
A love that was supposed to always last?

Now they live in separate homes of their own,
The children talk to their dad on the phone.
They do get to see him on weekends and holidays,
But that isn't the same as having Dad there always.

She hears a song and remembers back to a time that was good,
When they loved and laughed the way a married couple should.
She tries to figure out what went so terribly wrong,
To destroy a marriage that should have lasted so long.

He lies in bed and remembers a woman so soft and sweet,
Her hair that lay in curls down her back was the color of wheat.
She felt so good in his arms that it always made his heart ache,
Now with his life so empty he can feel his heart break.

This was love that should have lasted forever,
A love so strong that no one should be able to sever.
But love has to be guarded like a precious treasure,
So instead of pain it will continue to bring pleasure.

I Am God's Child

I am God's child and He made me,
Though far from perfect I may be.
He made each flaw with such tender care,
So when I see a mirror I won't sit and stare.

Instead I will see the people around,
I will see the problems that abound.
I will take the time to look deep in my heart,
To see how I can make their problems depart.

God did not make me fair of face,
Nor did he make me full of grace.
So that I will appreciate the beauty He made,
And in my eyes His glory will never fade.

I will appreciate the beauty of a little child,
And the graceful moves of animals of the wild.
The blossoms of the flowers in the spring,
Will always make my heart want to sing.

The sunshine will always make me smile,
To feel its warmth against my skin for a while.
I will notice how the roses glisten in a lovely way,
After a cool soaking rain on a hot summer day.

Because I'm not perfect I will always see,
When a friend needs a hug just from me.
And when there is something I can do,
To help a stranger that is in need too.

Because I'm not filled with too much pride,
I will try harder never to be hurtful or snide.
Without my flaws I would have missed so much love,
So for all of these blessings I thank God above.

What Women Want

It feels so good all snuggled down in bed,
With the covers up over my head.
Then the alarm clock rings and disturbs my sleep,
Sometimes I just want to weep.

I give a groan and crawl out of bed,
I know I have to work to buy my bread.
I stumble to the kitchen with my eyes shut tight,
Not yet willing to let in the harsh morning light.

I'm just sure I'm not up to going to work today,
But then again there are all of those bills to pay.
I find the coffee and fill up a cup with the warm brew,
Hoping somehow the coffee will help me renew.

To my surprise my eyes open up,
And that was after just one cup.
I stretch, yawn and am ready to begin the day,
Dressed and with another cup I'm on my way.

The day was busy and before I knew,
I was wondering where the day flew.
It was late afternoon and I was getting tired,
If I didn't get some energy I was going to be fired.

Chocolate was what I needed and what I craved,
I went through my purse and found a piece I had saved.
As I let that chocolate melt slowly on my tongue,
Once again I felt refreshed and suddenly young.

I got all my work done before it was due,
Three more pieces of chocolate helped me get through.
After a hard day at work it was time to go home to rest,
As long as I have coffee and chocolate I can do my best.

One-Step Away

From the day you are born you are one-step away,
To the next stage of your life day by day.
One-step away from crawling and walking,
One-step away from running and talking.

From the first day of kindergarten and all through school,
You begin learning life's lessons and the Golden Rule.
Important lessons like how to be a good friend,
And when to be strong and when to be willing to bend.

You will learn when to work and when to play,
And how to balance it out in just the right way.
You will learn how to handle life's disappointments,
And how to be proud of your accomplishments.

One day you will be one-step from your first date,
Life will have taught you how to choose the right mate.
So you can live your married life loving each other,
Then you will be one-step from being a mother.

One-step away from feeling your heart fill with pride,
As you look at the beautiful children by your side.
One-step away from watching them blossom and grow,
You will love them more than they will ever know.

The children grow up and move out on their own,
The pain in your heart is one like you've never known.
The house feels so empty and quiet now,
Life will go on, but you're not sure how.

But you are one-step away from grandchildren sitting in your lap,
You get to spoil them all you want and put them down for a nap.
You can send them home when they are fussy and cry,
And look forward to the next time they decide to come by.

Years pass by and your husband retires,
You have time to fill life's dreams and desires.
You sit and you talk of what the future holds,
And talk of the past as you watch your life unfold.

Then one dreadful day your husband gets ill,
When he dies you know that it was God's will.
You are overcome with pain and grief,
Your time together was far too brief.

Each year is lonelier than the year before,
Each day you seem to miss him even more.
Heaven is where your dear husband will reside,
But you are just one-step from being back by his side.

Hope

Hope is when abused, neglected children fight,
To make it to adulthood and live their lives right.
They don't repeat the mistakes of their father and mother,
Through kindness they teach their children to love one another.

Hope is when hungry children work hard to learn,
So they can get a good job with a good salary to earn.
They will have food and a roof over their heads,
Their children will have blankets and cozy beds.

Hope is when you send your boy off to war,
To fight for what this great country stands for.
Hope makes you believe he will come home again,
To live a full life and become an old man.

Hope is when a farmer plants his seed,
To grow the food his family will need.
And when the ground is cracked and dry,
That soon the rain will fall from the sky.

Hope helps us make it through life's way,
Especially when troubles darken our day.
It brings us sunshine when problems rain,
It brings us comfort through our pain.

Country Road

I walk along a country road winding through trees,
With the sound of birds floating on a warm breeze.
The trees meet over the road to make an arch of green,
The beauty and peace is like none you have ever seen.

Beautiful wildflowers of all kinds cover the ground,
Every color of the rainbow in the flowers can be found.
Bright colors aren't the only thing that the flowers wear,
The scent of their perfume gently drifts through the air.

The beautiful sounds of the earth fill my ears,
The simple sounds that God intends us to hear.
The buzzing of the bees while they are making honey,
Is not a pleasure that can be bought with money.

A squirrel chatters from the top of a tree,
Trying to keep his acorns away from me.
The sound of the birds building their nest,
Trying to find the twigs that will work best.

I walk along that dusty road in bare feet,
Another person I will not meet.
Alone in that quiet place I'll rejoice,
For I will be able to hear God's voice.

God will let me know what he expects,
And I will have time on my life to reflect.
The beauty and peace will fill my soul,
With God in my life, my life will be whole.

Always take time to walk those long country roads,
Where a busy life with no time seem to have slowed.
Take time to enjoy the beauty and the sound,
Your spirit will soar at God's creations all around.

The Love of a Dog

A woman lost her husband and was all alone,
She had no one to talk to, not even on the phone.
One day a little Pomeranian came to live with her,
With big brown eyes and a bundle of soft fur.

The pup was so tiny and had such a sweet little face,
The woman named her Dolly and gave her an embrace.
Dolly was just a puppy and took a lot of care,
The woman didn't have time for sadness or despair.

She would always miss her husband every single day,
But the pup had to be fed and taken care of in every way.
Potty training a puppy is not all that easy,
That also kept the woman very busy.

Now Dolly is older and has become a friend,
She will be a companion to the very end.
Dolly is very spoiled, but her loyalty is real,
It is love that the woman and the little dog feel.

Dolly follows her around the house wherever she goes,
And when she picks Dolly up she gets kissed on the nose.
When nighttime comes and it is time to go to bed.
Dolly's snuggled up by the woman on the bedspread.

The little dog's expressive face brings joy to the woman,
A happiness that she never knew she would have again.
Dolly can look mischievous, sweet, sad, or even a little put out.
When she lays her little ears back you know she ready to pout.

The little dog gives the woman a reason to live,
Because of Dolly she stays healthy and active.
She has someone to talk to throughout the day,
And Dolly always listens to everything she has to say.

Music of Nature

Music makes you feel happy, sad, or sentimental,
The sounds can create moods so soft and gentle.
Music can make toes tap and anxious to dance,
It makes sweethearts ready for a night of romance.

Music comes from instruments or someone who sings,
But the best music is the music that nature brings.
The wind rustling through the leaves makes a lovely sound,
And when the wind moans, a song in a minor key can be found.

The bubbling brook makes the music of laughter,
As it skips over the rocks racing to the sea thereafter.
The birds in the treetops sing songs so sweet,
That it makes the morning a pleasure to greet.

A symphony orchestra is played when it rains,
It starts out slowly and then the speed gains.
The rain pours harder and the volume is heightening,
And the music crescendos with thunder and lightening.

The crickets chirping in the night serenade,
With their tiny legs the music is played.
They play music like a violin with a bow,
Moving their little legs to and fro.

Music of any kind is good for the soul,
It brings you peace and makes you whole.
All music is beautiful but the very best,
Is the music of nature by which we are blessed.

All Kinds of Love

Love is a very special word that can mean many things,
From the pleasure of chocolate to the love a sweetheart brings.
No matter how the word love is used it is very appealing,
And it always leaves people with a warm feeling.

A cup of hot chocolate on a cold winter day,
Hot bubble baths to ease the stress of life away,
A long walk through the peaceful countryside,
Are the simplest forms of love that abide.

The special love for a pet is like no other,
And the devotion they feel for one another.
No matter what happens, they never judge,
And they never ever hold a grudge.

Love is also shared with a friend,
Someone on whom you can always depend,
The secrets and laughter they share,
With someone who will always care.

Then there is the love of a sweetheart,
Where two lovers never want to part.
The love grows and blossoms like a flower,
Slowly gaining in strength and power.

A special love of a mother for her child,
Is a love so gentle, sweet, and mild.
It is also extremely powerful and strong,
So it can protect the child from any wrong.

There is one love more special than any of the rest,
The love that God fills our soul with is the very best.
It is a love full of compassion, comfort, and hope,
A very special love that will help us in hard times to cope.

Rainbows

Rainbows are magical and full of mystery,
With stories that started way back in history.
Stories of leprechauns and pots of gold,
And of flying unicorns are still being told.

In a sky that has been so dark and gray,
And filled with rain throughout the day.
Then the bright colors make a sparkling bow,
Giving new hope for the day to those below.

The beauty and hope that the rainbow brings,
Makes the imagination take off on wings.
The mystical beauty makes you think of magical lands,
Up past the clouds where a colorful castle stands.

A place where good always overcomes evil,
Like white knights in times medieval.
There a beautiful princess that is in distress,
Is saved by the knight so his love he can profess.

Beyond the rainbow is a place for dreams,
Among the raindrops sparkling in sunbeams.
We know our lives will have hope and cheer,
For after the rain a rainbow will appear.

The Perfect World

The perfect world would be full of peace,
All fights and wars would suddenly cease.
People would treat each other with respect,
Instead of the rudeness that people expect.

People would greet each other with a smile,
That brightened someone's day for a while.
Children would not be disrespectful,
Because their parents had been neglectful.

Road rage would be a thing of the past,
Drivers wouldn't mind if they were last.
There would be no more jesters that shouldn't be,
Just a friendly smile and a wave for them to see.

Even though the world is a busy place,
A stranger would be a friendly face.
Always willing to help someone in need,
Willing to stop to do a good deed.

There would be no murder or no crime,
Doors wouldn't have to be locked all the time.
Children would be safe playing out in the yard,
Schools wouldn't need a security guard.

This would be a perfect world if love could abound,
And if everyone smiled instead of frowned.
If everyone just put their selfishness behind,
A perfect world they just might find.

Long Ago

Long ago people took time to take pleasure,
From the world like it was a special treasure.
They worked and played through their life,
Together the family handled all the strife.

They greeted the morning in the same way,
When the sun peeked through their window each day.
They would smile at the sight of the bright sunshine,
Knowing that the day would be sunny and fine.

The family worked together as one,
Fun came only after the work had been done.
Even as they worked, talked, and shared,
Everyone knew that the others cared.

Everyone sat down together at all meals,
For laughter and talk of how everyone feels.
Problems are shared and decisions made,
And before they ate they held hands and prayed.

When the work's done and the sun sets low in the sky,
They sat on the porch and listened to the whippoorwills cry.
Mother snapped beans to get ready for canning,
Dad talked about the work he was planning.

The children were chasing fireflies in the night,
Putting them in jars so they could see their light.
The parents watched their children with care,
Laughing at their antics as they played in the fresh air.

This is a time for the family to unwind,
To get a break from work and the daily grind.
They count the sparkling stars up in the sky,
Singing songs and telling stories to help time pass by.

After a kiss and a bedtime story was read,
It was time for the children to be in bed.
Mother listened to their prayers as they kneeled,
At the sight her heart with pride was filled.

She went back and sat with her husband for a while,
They talked of all the things that made their life worthwhile.
There were problems and there always would be,
But together they would handle each problem they see.

Alone in the night they were sweethearts once more,
She was once again the young woman he would always adore.
They knew that even though life is hard sometimes,
They would love each other through the good and bad times.

The Artist

The blank white canvas to most looks empty and clean,
But the artist's mind begins to see a beautiful scene.
The artist begins to see majestic mountains and gentle streams,
And a field of wildflowers where the sunlight gleams.

The artist gets out a palette and tubes of paint she will need,
And with a variety of brushes she is ready to proceed.
Good lighting is always something the artist must include,
And some soft romantic music helps to set the mood.

The top of the canvas is painted a summer blue,
With white fluffy clouds floating through.
Then the artist takes paint and a palette knife,
And a range of mountains suddenly takes life.

Trees adorn the canvas with shades of green,
A quiet little stream makes the picture quite serene.
A little log cabin is set among the trees,
A boat is in the water rocking with the breeze.

Through the trees the sunlight touches the ground,
It's in that area that the wildflowers can be found.
Near the stream the artist paints a deer,
Listening closely to make sure no man is near.

The artist stops for a moment to sit and gaze,
She has been painting all day as if in a daze.
The artist wonders where this painting came from,
And knows it was not from her that it had come.

The artist stares at the painting and has no doubt,
It was because of God that this painting came about.
He gave her this talent so with others she can share,
The beauty God gave us that's so beautiful and rare.

An Unmarried Woman

There was a woman who lived all alone,
She taught school, but had no children of her own.
She had two dogs and did her very best,
To try to fill the house and her empty nest.

She was a girl that had been quite shy and demure,
A girl that had been taught to live a life that was pure.
She was raised always to be good and kind,
Even to strangers and stray animals she might find.

She led a very quiet life in the country home,
And never very far from home did she roam.
She was young and innocent for her many years,
Because she was so shy dating was one of her fears.

So she lived her quiet little life in a very simple way,
By enjoying the world God gave her each and every day.
She loved working in gardens and taking care of pets,
Taking long walks through the woods and watching sunsets.

The young woman filled her life with music and art,
She loved her family and friends with all her heart.
The woman worked at church where her spirit has grown,
And she loved the children at school as if they were her own.

When the woman looks up to count the stars in the sky,
And counts her many blessing she gives a sigh.
She filled her life with the best things God has to give,
And this young woman definitely has a reason to live.

Harvest Moon

I look up at the harvest moon so bright,
And gaze at the beautiful orange moonlight,
The stars are twinkling around the moon in the sky,
It looks like a lantern with fireflies fluttering by.

I sit in the dark in the cool fresh air,
Enjoying the beauty that I see there.
In the silence I enjoy the peace,
As I watch the number of stars increase.

The moment is so magical that I wish upon a star,
Even though at my age I know that is bizarre.
Smiling down at me is the man in the moon,
It is beautiful enough to make me swoon.

The problems of the day seem to disappear,
And I begin to think of all the things I hold dear.
The weariness I felt earlier now is gone,
Replaced with new energy so I can face the dawn.

Magic of Childhood

The magic of childhood is a wonderful thing,
There is no limit to what their imagination can bring.
Their world is always filled with excitement and fun,
It is sad that the magic ends when our childhood is done.

Tooth fairies that slip under their pillows at night,
To replace a tooth with a shiny coin in the moonlight.
Easter bunnies come in the early dawn,
With colorful eggs that they hide on the lawn.

At Christmas they just know they can hear on the roof,
Santa's sleigh and the pawing of a reindeer hoof.
Santa sliding down the chimney is possible in their mind,
To put the toys in their stockings for them to find.

At night when the children are fast asleep,
All of their toys come to life and out they creep.
The toys play games all through the night,
And go back to being just toys at the morning light.

Pine straw can be made into a giant bird nest,
As they pretend to be baby birds needing their rest.
Little cowboys also made a fort with pine straw,
To protect them from any of the dangers they saw.

A pile of sand becomes a castle with kings and knights,
A moat surrounds the kingdom to protect it from fights.
Pretend alligators live in the castle's moat,
So an enemy can't get to the castle in a boat.

It is such a shame that all the magic disappears,
When we become adults and a life of problems appears.
We could use a little magic to help us along life's way,
To lighten our load and brighten our dreary day.

The Tree

The tree was just a little twig,
It was very thin and not very big.
It was planted in the backyard with care,
In hope that someday fruit it would bear.

The family watered it and watched it grow,
Through the years the progress was slow.
The tree was thin although it did grow tall,
It was healthy even though it was small.

Through the years the tree grew thick and strong,
The limbs branched out and became very long.
Leaves covered the tree to shade the ground from the heat,
It was a wonderful place for the family to retreat.

In the midst of the limbs the birds built their nest,
Feeding baby birds who constantly protest.
All are claiming they are the next one to be fed,
The poor mama bird is ready to put them to bed.

The tree grows up high into the sky,
And produces pecans in good supply.
The squirrels get ready for winter by gathering food,
Although on most of the nuts they stopped and chewed.

The fall comes and the leaves change to yellow and red,
They cover the ground like a blanket on a bed.
The limbs are bare and winter is on its way,
The animals find shelter and a warm place to stay.

Snow covers the bare limbs and turns them white,
The tree glistens in the morning sunlight.
How exciting it will be when the family sees,
The spring being announced by little green leaves.

An Old-Fashioned Woman

I should have been born in a century of the past,
For I'm quite old-fashioned and would fit in at last.
I believe children should be innocent and sweet,
And they should make their parents' lives complete.

I believe that marriage is forever and a day,
Couples discuss their problems until they go away.
They don't get a divorce because of hard times or a fight,
They work on their marriage to make it good and right.

I believe a family should spend time together,
Meals are a time that families should always gather.
Families should talk and share things about their day,
All family members should get a turn to have their say.

I believe that people should always treat others with respect,
Kindness from your neighbor is what you should expect.
Bad language should be something that is never used,
And little children should never be neglected or abused.

A lady should be gentle, pure and kind,
Strong when needed and yet remain refined.
A man should treat his lady as a very rare pearl,
Knowing that she was his completely and his only girl.

Marriage between the two lovers should come before the babies do,
Kissing should be the only thing that comes before marriage too.
Dancing should be a beautiful and graceful event,
A chance to get to touch, but it should be kept decent.

I know my thoughts are not popular or even normal for today,
The world has changed and I'm considered old-fashioned for my way.
I know there are many that would strongly disagree,
But I definitely believe that God agrees with me.

Little Boys

When your boy comes home check to see if he's followed by a stray dog,
And check all of his pockets for lizards, bugs, or maybe even a frog.
When his mother sees that mischievous grin and a twinkle in his eye,
She should know that there is a spider crawling around close by.

When a boy gets too quiet it is always time to go see,
What he is doing and where he might be.
When boys get too quiet it is always a time to beware,
They are usually thinking up some prank so special and rare.

Little boys like to run, jump, and climb,
And they like to eat and have a good time.
They tear big holes in the knees of their jeans,
Unfortunately that lasts into their teens.

One minute the boys are mad and in a big fight,
Throwing punches and kicking with all of their might.
After the fight they're best friends and ready to play,
So with a baseball and bat they have fun the rest of the day.

With wiggly worms little boys fish in the lake,
But they are just as happy if they catch a big snake.
If they don't catch anything they tie a rope to a tree,
And swing over the lake splashing with glee.

At the end of the day their clothes are wet, dirty, or muddy,
If their mother is lucky their knee isn't skinned or bloody.
The boys comes running through the house with a smile on their face,
And grab some food as they go back outside to finish the race.

After it is dark and the little boy has been put to bed,
Goodnight kisses have been given and a story has been read.
The little boy is asleep leaving the mother there by his side,
She brushes a strand hair out of his eyes as her heart fills with pride.

He looks so angelic as he sleeps so peacefully in the night,
She knows she has to treasure each moment with all her might.
These youthful years of fun and joy will quickly fly by,
And in its place will be a man in a blink of an eye.

The Old Days

Women used to wash the laundry in a stream on the rocks,
They didn't buy clothes they sewed and knitted socks.
There were no such things as dryers to put your clothes in,
You hung them on a line outside and attached them with a pin.

Vegetables were not bought in a grocery store,
They grew large gardens which was quite a chore.
Gardens had to be tended and vegetables canned,
Meals for the whole year had to be planned.

Milk for the family came from the family cow,
It didn't come in jugs from stores as it does now.
The cream from the milk was put in a churn,
To make enough butter everyone took a turn.

Afternoons were spent on the porch shelling beans and peas,
The porch was the coolest place catching the summer breeze.
There was no air conditioner, television, or radio,
Music came late in the afternoon with a fiddle and a bow.

Eggs were gathered from the hens for breakfast everyday,
Old hens were eaten when they were too old to lay.
Animals were raised on the land so there would be meat,
This provided another way for the family to eat.

There were no cars traveling the world around,
Horses' hooves and rattling carts were the only sound.
Families mostly stayed at home unless they had to go,
To the closest town to sell some of the things they grow.

The room was lit by lanterns all through the night,
Children's homework was done by the lantern's light.
The family went to bed early because they got up with the sun,
They need their rest every night for work, school, and fun.

Life was hard and lived by the sweat of the brow,
I suppose that life seems much easier now.
But did we lose something very special along the way,
Where families enjoyed spending time together each day?

Two Little Girls

The little girls have a tea party and spill the tea on the rug,
When a big brother comes in and scares them with a bug.
Mother comes in to kill the bug and clean up the mess,
She does her best to calm the girls who are in distress.

The girls put a bandage on the knee of their doll,
They call each other using play phones to make the call.
They dress up in mother's old clothes and wear high-heeled shoes,
The shoes make them stumble and fall and they get a bruise.

The girls put the dolls to bed and go outside to play,
They decide to pick wildflowers and make a pretty bouquet.
On the swings the little girls try to swing up high,
In their little minds they can reach up to the sky.

When they tire of swinging they make mud pies in the dirt,
They make apple, peach, and chocolate pies for dessert.
The girls brush off the dirt and play hide and seek,
The girls try very hard not to cheat and peek.

They make a playhouse under the old oak tree,
One is the mother the other is the little baby.
The baby keeps running off and mother has to run,
To catch the baby and bring it home to have more fun.

It's time for church so the other girl has to go home,
Time for the mothers to untangle curls with a comb.
Bathed and dressed in pink lace they look so sweet,
If only their mothers can keep them so clean and neat.

At church they are together with each other once more,
They spot each other as soon as they are in the door.
Although they sometimes giggle, they are really pretty good,
And behave in church the way good little girls should.

The day is finally over and has been full of fun,
A day filled with all the things the little girls have done.
It was a special childhood day filled with fun and laughter,
A day the two little girls will remember forever after.

The Little Cloud

The little white cloud floated high in the sky,
Watching the birds as they flew by.
It basked in the sunshine all through the day,
As it made puffy little shapes along the way.

The little white cloud looked down below,
And saw a man in his garden with a hoe.
The man was sweating and very hot,
While weeding the vegetables in his little plot.

The little white cloud blocked the sun from the man,
To make a cool shade for him was the cloud's plan.
The man straightened up and smiled up at the cloud,
And the smile from the man made the little cloud proud.

The warm sun made the water evaporate,
The little cloud got heavy with the weight.
Then the little cloud looked down at earth and saw,
Crime, abuse, neglect, and people breaking the law.

It made the little cloud very angry and sad,
To see the people act so disrespectful and bad.
The little cloud turned dark and very gray,
And the little cloud began to cry that day.

Thunder boomed and lightening lit up the sky,
And with anger and sadness the cloud continued to cry,
Until it looked down at the earth once more,
And saw a man help a lost child back to his front door.

The little cloud stopped crying at the compassionate sight,
The lightening and the thunder grew quiet in the night.
The moon was able to shine and show its face,
The stars were able to twinkle with style and grace.

The weather got cooler and the little cloud shakes,
Instead of rain the little cloud was dropping snowflakes.
The snow mounts up higher and deeper on the ground,
And everything is so quiet that there is not a sound.

The children are delighted by the sight of the snow,
They grab their sleds and out the door they go.
Snowmen and snow angels are made through the day,
Giggles from children can be heard as they play.

The sun comes out and the snowmen slowly melt,
The warmth from the sunshine can be felt.
The little cloud looks down and sees leaves on the trees,
The birds are flying by gliding on the breeze.

The little cloud knows that the cycle is starting over,
As it sees the ground being covered by clover.
The little cloud sees all that happens down below,
It knows when things die and when they grow.

Friendship

Friendship happens when two spirits meet,
It is a warm feeling making you feel complete.
Age, race, or gender does not seem to matter,
Nor does it depend on whether you're thin or fatter.

Friendship doesn't rely on whether you are poor or have money,
Neither does it depend on whether you are serious or funny.
It doesn't seem to matter how attractive or even how smart,
One friend can like sports and the other can like art.

Friendship occurs when two souls find something special that they share,
Or it may be their differences making a friendship so rare.
Friends know what your faults and flaws are but don't seem to care,
They know your talents and your strengths and problems you bear.

A friend will listen to you rant and rave when you need to let off steam,
They will encourage you along the way to reach your highest dream.
A friend will always be there with a shoulder for you to cry on,
And lean on them when you are weak and your strength is gone.

Friends will laugh together until tears stream down their face,
Laughter between friends seems to help problems be erased.
No matter if you're right or wrong a friend will always love you,
But if they think you're wrong they will let you know that too.

If you have some true friends be sure that they are treasured,
For the worth of a true friend can never be measured.
Friends are worth more than any pearls or gold,
And the value of a friend only increases as it grows old.

Age of Time

With age comes wisdom and so you should be proud,
When you have to announce your age in front of a crowd.
You have worked long and hard to get where you are,
Without years of experience you wouldn't have gotten this far.

Do not be ashamed of the wrinkles on your face,
They are like the delicate lines of a spider web or in fine lace.
Wrinkles show your life through the good times and the bad,
There are smile lines when you're happy and frown lines when you're sad.

You may have a little tummy because of the children you have had,
So just think of your beautiful family and you will suddenly feel glad.
When your child looks up with a beautiful smile meant just for you,
The weight won't seem to matter so much and you will not be blue.

Think of the trials and troubles of life and you will be assured,
That you would not want to repeat the problems you have endured.
Be thankful for the age of time that you have made it through,
For through the trials and trouble there has been much pleasure too.

Just the Way You Are

I love you just the way you are,
You are my light and guiding star.
You are my strength when I grow weak,
And you are my hope when things look bleak.

When I am tired you give me rest,
With a home that's a cozy little nest.
When I am scared you are always there,
To make me feel safe and without a care.

If I accomplish something new,
You're as proud as if you accomplished it too.
You lift my spirits when I am down,
By making me laugh when you see me frown.

You are so very special to me,
My love for you goes deeper than the sea.
Don't ever think you need to change a thing,
My love for you makes my heart sing.

You are my world both night and day,
With you my life is complete in every way.
When you look up and see a shooting star,
Remember that I love you just the way you are.

My Favorite Things

When troubles and problems arise through the day,
I close my eyes and let my mind wander away.
I think of all my favorite things,
And the pleasure and comfort it brings.

I see white daisies in a green field,
And sandcastles that children build.
I see purple violets growing wild,
And the beautiful smile of a child.

I think of a bubble bath that smells so sweet,
Afterwards hot chocolate is a special treat.
Trees in the spring when they first bud out,
With bright green leaves when they begin to sprout.

Long walks through the woods on a summer day,
With my dogs running ahead to lead the way.
The sky in the evening turning pink and blue,
Makes the sunset a beautiful view.

Watching a bird teach her babies to fly,
Soon they will soar up high in the sky.
A full moon that sheds so much light,
You can walk around out in the night.

Little girls in dresses with ribbons in their hair,
And patent leather shoes polished with such care.
A sleeping child is such a beautiful sight,
They look like an angel just kissed them goodnight.

These images bring such peace to my mind,
That the problems I had seemed harder to find.
When I think of some of my favorite things,
My spirit feels lighter as if it's grown wings.

The Wallflower

A young girl sits all alone with a cup of punch,
She sits against the wall away from the other bunch.
No one seems to notice that the girl is even there,
On either side of her is an empty chair.

The others around her laugh, dance, and sing,
In the room the sounds of happiness ring.
Music fills the room and makes the girl's toes tap,
When the dance is over all the people clap.

She smiles when someone appears to look her way,
But they never speak or have anything to say.
She would have given anything to join in the fun,
And dance the night away the way the others had done.

The girl didn't know what to say,
When a young man did look her way.
The young girl felt awkward and very shy,
So she just watched the dancers whirl by.

She saw a boy on whom she had a crush,
Come sit beside her and she felt herself blush.
He asked her for the very next dance,
She felt as if she were in a trance.

They whirled around the dance room floor,
And then he asked her for one dance more.
Then the party is over and they turn out the light,
And he asks her if he can walk her home in the night.

He walks with her holding her hand,
And talks about the music and the band.
Walking under the stars and the moon,
They reach her house all too soon.

She looks up into his beautiful blue eyes,
As they say their final goodbyes.
Before he leaves he gives her a kiss,
This was truly a night of bliss.

I Wish for You

I look down at my sleeping child,
She looks so sweet and meek and mild.
I think about what I wish for you,
Not only now but for your future too.

I wish for you that all wars would cease,
So you could grow up in a world of peace.
A place where there is no crime,
And you don't have to be afraid all the time.

I wish for you all the beautiful things,
The beautiful things that nature brings.
Plenty of sunshine and summer showers,
That make rainbows and bouquets of flowers.

I wish for you to be kind and good,
To treat people with compassion the way you should.
I want you to treat everyone with respect,
So the good things of life you can expect.

I wish for you all the love the world has to give,
So happiness will fill the life that you live.
I want you to always freely give love,
To family, friends, and God above.

I wish for you always to be wise,
When problems and conflicts in your life arise.
Be quick to forgive and slow to anger,
And you will avoid sorrow and danger.

If all of these things come about,
Then I will have no room for doubt.
That the world will love you as I do,
And God will always be with you.

The Kitten

A small gray kitten is born in a barn,
In a grassy spot near a field of corn.
The little kitten still lives on its mother's milk,
Its little claws are like needles and its hair like silk.

Soon the kitten was ready to climb and run,
There were so many ways to have some fun.
The barn had places to search and hide,
And when tired she curled up by her mother's side.

A man came and picked up the kitten one day,
He put her in his pickup and drove away.
He put the kitten in a cage small and bare,
Then he turned and left her there.

The poor little kitten had nothing to do,
There were no stalls full of hay to search through.
She wanted her mother to curl up by,
And through the long night she began to cry.

One day a lady came and looked down at her,
Then picked her up to rub her soft fur.
When she put the kitten up close to her shoulder,
The world suddenly seemed a little less colder.

The lady took the kitten with her that day,
Once again she was put in a car and driven away.
This time though she went to a home,
Where she was free to play and roam.

Now the kitten sleeps in a bed,
Curled up by the woman's head.
There are toys to play with and things to do,
And plenty of love for the kitten too.

Fall

I should be happy in the fall with leaves of red and yellow,
But instead I am sad and feel somewhat mellow.
I watch the leaves fall from the trees,
Floating to the ground on a gentle breeze.

The beautiful leaves of red, yellow, and gold,
Show me the summer leaves are dead and old.
They look like a patchwork blanket covering the ground,
Walking across them makes a crunching sound.

The limbs on the trees look harsh and bare,
Without the leaves they normally wear.
The days are short and the nights are long,
And you no longer hear the bluebirds' song.

It is cold during the morning and the night,
The sun does not shed as much light.
When you go outside you need a sweater,
To make the weather a little better.

The pecans are ready and apples are ripe,
So are oranges and pumpkins of every type.
The air is crisp during the day,
The field is full of bales of hay.

The grass has died back and the flowers are gone,
No dewdrops sparkle on roses in the early dawn.
The colors of pink, purple, and blue,
Have changed to orange and brown too.

I know that winter is close behind,
And a warm place will be hard to find.
Some of the animals will sleep the winter away,
Waiting for the first warm spring day.

I know fall to most is beautiful,
Fresh fruit and nuts are also plentiful.
But it always makes me a little sad,
To lose the beautiful things summer had.

Angel in Disguise

A stranger walked up to a big house,
Meek and mild and quiet as a mouse.
The stranger was dirty and dressed in rags,
All of his belongings were in two small bags.

When a young man answered the knock on the door,
The stranger asked for a crust of bread and no more.
The young man said, "I have work to do,
I'm far too busy to bother with you."

The door slammed in the stranger's face,
He shook his head sadly as he left that place.
He walked to the next house made of brick,
The hedges around the house were full and thick.

A woman opened the door and with a look of disgust,
Said, "Leave or I will call the police if I must."
She never even asked why he was there,
But then again, she didn't really care.

The stranger walked on down the lane,
To a house that was small and plain.
The house needed painting and many repairs,
Poverty is what this little house wears.

A woman comes out with a little boy behind,
They smile at the stranger that they find.
When he ask for a crust of bread,
She invites him in to be fed.

She explains that her husband has died,
And they don't have much she said as she sighed.
She told him he could share their meager meal,
All she had were a few beans, but he could eat his fill.

The stranger sat at the table with them,
They laughed, ate, and talked with him.
They all shared the beans from that one small pot,
Resenting him for eating was never given a thought.

The stranger thanked her and started to leave,
And then the woman grabbed him by the sleeve.
She had been saving two slices of bread,
He must take it for later the woman said.

She wished she could give more but it was all that she had,
Life had just been hard since her boy lost his dad.
The boy ran up with a smile and took the stranger's hand,
And gave him his blanket for warmth as he traveled the land.

The man thanked them both with tears in his eyes,
Patted the boy on the head and said his final goodbyes.
As he reached the door he turned and smiled,
And said "God bless you my dear beautiful child."

When they looked the man had disappeared,
Just vanished in thin air or so it appeared.
The woman and boy just closed the door,
And didn't think about it anymore.

Then one day her yard was full of men,
There were also quite a few women.
The men had paint and tools of every kind,
The woman had all of the food they could find.

They told the woman a man in rags,
Had given the church two little bags.
He told them of the woman's needs,
And also of their kind deeds.

The stranger said the bags would supply,
Everything they would need to buy.
They could help the woman and her son,
With all the things that needed done.

They looked in the bags and found a bar of gold,
It was shiny but looked quite old.
They discovered when they turned around,
That the stranger was nowhere to be found.

They filled the house with food that was good,
And repaired the house to look as it should.
So who was this stranger that entered their lives,
Was it really an angel in disguise?

A Soldier's Life

A soldier who is proud and brave,
Willing to sacrifice his life to save,
Our freedoms we have gotten used to,
For the USA and the red, white, and blue.

The soldier is also a man with a wife,
That he loves and would protect with his life.
With each year their love has grown,
And it breaks his heart to leave her alone.

He looks at his daughter that he will leave,
The thought of returning to a young woman makes him grieve.
He can already see her blossoming like a little flower,
The thought of boys coming leaves a taste that is sour.

He should be there for her very first date,
To look the boy in the eye so he would know his fate.
The boy would know what to expect,
If he didn't treat his little girl with respect.

He turns his attention to his small son,
By the time he's back Little League will be done.
He won't get to go to one single game,
They will write but it won't be the same.

When he learns to ride a bike his dad won't be there,
This will be one more event he won't be able to share.
He will miss playing ball in the backyard,
He must appear strong, but all of this is so hard.

His wife's stomach is big and round,
He will have another son the sonogram found.
He will not be there for the birth,
For he will be on the other side of the earth.

This son will not know his voice or his face,
He won't even know Dad belongs in this place.
He won't be there when he learns to walk,
Or even when he begins to talk.

His wife is trying to smile for his sake,
Even though her heart is about to break.
She won't have him by her side,
And her tears are hard to hide.

The day he leaves they say their goodbyes,
He hugs his wife and she cries.
They talk of the day when he will be back with them,
Knowing in their hearts this may be the last time they see him.

Why I Write

If I write something to make you smile,
My time spent writing will be worthwhile.
If I can write something to make your load lighter,
Then I can make your future a little brighter.

If my words can give you hope,
Maybe I can give you a way to cope.
If my poems can make you a better friend,
A relationship might be on the mend.

I'd like to write something to help you renew,
A relationship with a spouse meant just for you.
Maybe I can write something so you can see,
How true love is supposed to be.

I hope to write something to keep your dreams alive,
Or to love and appreciate your children when they arrive.
I write so you'll see the beauty nature has to give,
And how people of the past used to live.

I wish for you hope and peace,
And beauty that will never cease.
I wish for you all the love,
From family, friends, and God above.